I SURVIVED

THE CHILDREN'S BLIZZARD, 1888

I SURVIVED

THE DESTRUCTION OF POMPEII, AD 79

THE AMERICAN REVOLUTION, 1776

THE BATTLE OF GETTYSBURG, 1863

THE GREAT CHICAGO FIRE, 1871

THE SAN FRANCISCO EARTHQUAKE, 1906

THE SINKING OF THE *TITANIC*, 1912

THE SHARK ATTACKS OF 1916

THE *HINDENBURG* DISASTER, 1937

THE BOMBING OF PEARL HARBOR, 1941

THE NAZI INVASION, 1944

THE ERUPTION OF MOUNT ST. HELENS, 1980

THE ATTACKS OF SEPTEMBER 11, 2001

HURRICANE KATRINA, 2005

THE JAPANESE TSUNAMI, 2011

THE JOPLIN TORNADO, 2011

I SURVIVED

THE CHILDREN'S BLIZZARD, 1888

by Lauren Tarshis

illustrated by Scott Dawson

Scholastic Inc.

Text copyright © 2018 by Dreyfuss Tarshis Media Inc.

Illustrations copyright © 2018 Scholastic Inc.

Photos ©: p. 114: Solomon D. Butcher, 1886/The Granger Collection; p. 118: The Granger Collection; p. 120: Golbez/Wikimedia; p. 122: Jacoby's Art Gallery/Minnesota Historical Society

This book is being published simultaneously in hardcover by Scholastic Press.

ISBN 978-0-545-91977-7

26 25 24 23   24 25 26

Printed in the U.S.A.   40

First printing 2018

Designed by Yaffa Jaskoll

For David

CHAPTER 1

JANUARY 12, 1888
PRAIRIE CREEK, DAKOTA TERRITORY
AROUND 10:00 A.M.

A deadly blizzard raged across the prairie, and eleven-year-old John Hale was trapped in a frozen nightmare. The wind screamed in his ears as he staggered through the blinding snow. His whole body was numb.

The monster storm had come out of nowhere, a massive black cloud moving faster than a train.

The temperature plunged. The wind howled. And then,

Roooaar!

The sky exploded like a bomb, blasting snow and ice through the air.

Ground-up ice raked John's eyes like tiny claws. The furious wind pounded him, tore at him, spun him around. He felt like he was locked in a cage with a furious beast trying to rip him to pieces.

And then a screaming gust picked John up and slammed him down. He tried to rise to his feet, but the wind was too strong. Snow was piling on top of him, burying him in an icy grave.

John felt his flesh freezing on his bones. His body's warmth was seeping out of him, like blood leaking from an open wound.

John had never wanted to move west, to this wide-open prairie. He was a city kid, not a tough pioneer. And now the maniac wind was hissing in his ears, taunting him.

You're weak!
You'll never make it!
You're doomed!

That terrifying, evil wind was the last sound John heard as he was buried alive.

CHAPTER 2

John's little sister, Franny, had disappeared.

She and John were on their way to their school-house. They were halfway through the three-mile walk from their farm. They were following an old wagon trail that cut through the tall, golden grass.

Franny, who was five, had been skipping up ahead. John had been watching her blond braids flap up and down, like the wings of a happy yellow bird. Somehow he'd lost sight of her.

John sped up, looking all around. It was hard to see through the grass, which rose up so high it tickled his neck. A unicorn could be prancing by, and John wouldn't notice.

"Franny!" he shouted. "Where are you?"

Whoosh, said the wind. *Swish*, said the grass.

But no sign of Franny.

John sighed. She must be playing hide-and-seek, her favorite game. When Franny found a good spot, she'd sit there forever.

She was going to make them late. It was hard enough for John, going to a school where he had no friends. But his teacher, Miss Ruell, was mean.

He pictured her now, her hair stretched back in a bun, her eyes glaring through her little round glasses. She was young, and barely five feet tall. But she ruled over the schoolhouse like a Civil War general. John had never once seen her smile. When kids were late, Miss Ruell made them stay in for recess and memorize some boring poem.

Torture!

"Franny!" John shouted.

He stood on his tiptoes, peering into the distance. All he could see, in any direction, was wide-open prairie. It seemed to stretch out forever, an ocean made of grass.

He still couldn't get used to it, all this empty land.

John and Franny and their parents had moved

6

here to Dakota about a year ago, from Chicago. It wasn't John's idea; he'd been happy living in the city. But Ma and Pa were fed up with their dark little apartment, their cursing neighbors, and the noise and stink that rose up from the street.

For years Ma and Pa had been talking about moving out west and buying a farm. But John always figured that was just their crazy dream, like John wishing he could be a pitcher for the Chicago White Stockings, his favorite baseball team.

Pa didn't make much money, working at a cabinet shop. How could they ever afford to buy land for a farm?

Then Ma and Pa heard they could get land in a place called Dakota. It was thousands of miles of open space, west of Minnesota. Dakota wasn't a state, but it would be soon, folks said.

And the government wanted farmers to come. They were even giving away big plots of land — for free! All you had to do was build a farm and stay for five years. Then the land was yours forever.

For Ma and Pa, it was a dream come true.

"We're heading west!" Pa boomed.

"We'll be pioneers," Ma said.

John hoped the West would be like the places in his favorite adventure stories, with rivers filled with gold nuggets and brave sheriffs chasing after famous bank robbers like Billy the Kid.

Ma and Pa sold practically everything they owned. They traveled west by train — it took seven days to reach the edge of Dakota Territory. Then they bought a rickety wagon and an ox to pull it. John named the ox Shadow, after his favorite White Stockings pitcher, Shadow Pyle.

It was a two-day ride to the little town of Prairie Creek. If you could call it a town. Only about twenty families lived there, on little farms scattered across the prairie. The main street was a dusty strip of dirt with a general store on one side and a hardware store and tiny hotel on the other. John's family settled on a 160-acre piece of land about two miles outside of town.

There were no rivers of gold, no brave sheriffs. There wasn't even a bank for a guy like Billy the

Kid to rob. There was only empty space — and endless work.

John and Pa were sometimes out in the fields from dawn until dark. Ma hardly ever stopped scrubbing and cooking and sweeping. Franny's scrawny little arms had sprouted muscles from hauling buckets of water from the well.

And the weather! The roasting summer sun. The thunderstorms that blackened the skies. Winter days so cold your spit froze before it hit the ground. Blizzards that came out of nowhere. Last winter the snow piled up almost to their rooftop. Pa had to dig a tunnel to get from the house to the barn.

But for John, the worst part was the emptiness. He got a lonely feeling when he looked out over the prairie, an ache inside him. It felt like a cold wind blowing right through his chest.

John didn't belong here. He felt stranded in the middle of nowhere.

And now Miss Ruell was going to punish him for being late.

"Franny!"

But wait. What if Franny wasn't playing a game? She could have wandered too far into the grass and gotten lost. Last year a little boy from town disappeared. One minute he'd been chasing jackrabbits behind his family's house. The next minute he'd vanished.

John and Pa joined the big search, but the poor kid was never found. It was like the prairie had opened its grassy jaws and swallowed him whole.

John cupped his hands around his mouth and yelled at the top of his lungs.

"Franny!"

The grass swished. The wind moaned. A flock of geese honked across the bright blue sky.

But no sign of Franny.

CHAPTER 3

John was at the edge of panic, when a giggle rose from the grass just a few yards ahead.

Franny's freckled face popped up.

She grinned at him. "Boo!"

"Franny!"

"Tricked you!" she said.

"You didn't trick me," John lied. "I knew exactly where you were hiding."

"How did you know?" Franny asked with a frown.

"I could smell you," John said, wrinkling his nose. "You stink worse than Princess."

Princess was their cow. Franny had picked her name.

Actually, Franny smelled a little like apples and Ma's soap. But John needed to get even with her for scaring him.

Franny's smile fell away. Her eyes started to tear up.

"I do not stink!" she said.

"All right," John said. He hated to see Franny sad. "But don't do that again. I thought I lost you, Fran. You scared me."

Franny burst out laughing. "That's a funny joke, Johnny," she said. "I know you're never scared."

John's heart lifted a little. It was good having a little sister who thought he was brave.

They rushed the last mile to the schoolhouse, which was about a quarter mile past Main Street. It was just a small, unpainted building, more like an overgrown dollhouse than a school. The school was barely big enough to fit all fifteen students. The big and little kids squeezed together in the one room. Miss Ruell had to figure out how to teach all of them.

Luckily, John and Franny weren't late.

The schoolhouse door was still closed. Kids were milling around outside, waiting for the bell. Franny went to join a jump rope game. John looked around, wishing he had someone to talk to. Back in Chicago, he had more friends than he could count. Before school he and his pals would shoot marbles or bug the girls they liked.

But here, there were only three boys his age: Rex, Peter, and Sven. They'd been friendly to John last fall, when he was brand-new. But John always felt uneasy around them, afraid he would say something wrong and make a fool of himself. So he avoided them.

Now they mostly ignored John — or maybe it was John who ignored them. He wasn't sure. But what did it matter? He'd missed his chance. And anyway, they probably knew John didn't belong here. He had nothing in common with those tough pioneer boys.

Peter and Sven were standing nearby, rubbing the sleep from their eyes. But then Rex came sprinting toward them, and Peter and Sven perked right up. Rex wasn't funny like Peter. And he didn't have big muscles like Sven. He was quiet, and serious. But Rex was their leader, without a doubt. His family had been in Dakota longer than anyone.

Rex skidded to a stop, huffing and puffing.

"I found him!" Rex exclaimed, wiping the sweat from his forehead.

"Found who?" asked Peter.

"King Rattler!" Rex burst out.

The boys gasped. John's ears pricked up.

King Rattler was a huge rattlesnake that all the kids talked about. There were rattle-snakes everywhere in Dakota — stretching their gold-and-brown bodies out on rocks, slither-ing through the tall grass, curling up in haylofts. Of all the sounds of the prairie, nothing chilled John's blood more than the *shshshshsk shshshshsk shshshshsk* of a rattler shak-ing its tail.

Get away, get away, it was saying. *Get away or I'll kill you!*

And King Rattler wasn't just any rattlesnake.

He was the biggest and most vicious snake there was, a killer that had been terrorizing people for years.

John had never seen him, but he'd heard the guys telling stories. Most snakes bit only if you stepped on them by accident. King Rattler would chase you down, right to your door. He'd bite your horse and then leap up and sink his fangs into your neck.

Or so the guys said.

"I saw him at the creek," Rex went on, his voice rising. "I followed him! I found his den. I saw where he lives!"

"*You* found King Rattler's den?" Peter gasped.

This was big news. Folks had been searching for years, John had heard.

"There's a hole, a big, nasty hole, right under a rock," Rex said. "I saw him go in. I saw it with my own eyes!"

John shuddered as he imagined the snake. The glistening fangs. The pink needle tongue. The deathly yellow eyes.

"So now," Rex said, his eyes narrow and fierce. "We can kill King Rattler!"

"We'll be famous!" Peter hooted.

Sven grinned.

Rex looked over and saw that John was listening in. John flicked his eyes down. Too late, though. He'd been caught spying.

Now Peter and Sven were looking at him, too. John started to get up to move away.

But Rex took a step toward him.

"Wanna come?" he asked.

John looked up in surprise.

"Come where?" he stammered.

"With us," Rex said. "To kill King Rattler."

John blinked.

They wanted him to help kill a monster rattlesnake? That was the dumbest idea John had ever heard!

He opened his mouth to say *no, thanks*.

But the guys were looking at him hopefully, like they really did want him to come along. It had been so long since any kids had looked at him that way.

Almost without thinking, John leaned forward.

"Sure I would," he said.

CHAPTER 4

SIX DAYS LATER
SUNDAY, SEPTEMBER 25, 1887
AROUND NOON
JOHN'S HOUSE

Their morning chores were done. John, Franny, Ma, and Pa were back from church. Now they were sitting at the table for Ma's special Sunday meal — squirrel stew.

Sundays were the best. John didn't have to go school and usually the whole family took the day off from working. John would play cards with

Franny, or go out hunting with Pa. Some days, he'd spend a whole hour just sitting around and doing nothing, like a millionaire.

But today was the day he was meeting the guys at the creek to kill King Rattler. Of course, he hadn't told his parents the true plan for the afternoon. He'd said he was going fishing with his new friends.

"Good stew," Pa said as he sopped up the sauce with a hunk of fresh bread.

It did smell delicious. But John's stomach was twisted so tight he couldn't take a bite.

"I'm glad you like it," Ma said, flashing a smile at Pa. "I'll tell the cook."

"Ma!" Franny giggled. "You're the cook!"

Ma's big brown eyes widened in pretend surprise. "I thought I was the queen!"

"Of course you're the queen!" Pa boomed. "And this is your castle."

Ma smiled, because their house was the complete opposite of a castle. It was just one small room, made of dirt.

Pa had built it for them when they got here last

fall. They wanted to live in a wooden house, but no trees grew in this part of Dakota. Pa couldn't just chop down a big oak and start sawing and hammering. And they couldn't afford to buy enough wood for a whole house.

So like most Dakota settlers, they built a house made of sod — dirt and grass peeled right up from the ground. Pa plowed up the sod in long strips, and then John helped him chop the strips into big blocks. They piled the blocks up to make the walls of their house. They had just enough money to buy some wood for the door and the roof.

The house — a "soddy" — was one small room, barely big enough for their beds, the table and chairs, and the big black stove that cooked their food and kept them warm in the winter. When it rained hard, muddy water dripped down from the ceiling. The dirt floor turned into a mud puddle. Worms and spiders and mice popped out of the walls.

But most of the time the soddy was

surprisingly cozy. The thick dirt walls helped keep the heat in during the winter. On oven-hot summer days the soddy stayed cool. And when they were all sitting together like they were now, with one of Ma's delicious meals on the table, the little dirt house felt like home.

Ma cleared away the stew bowls and brought out a berry pie. The sweet and buttery smell rose up. But John was too queasy to even have a taste.

He kept imagining how it would feel to have King Rattler's fangs stab into his flesh. The bite wasn't the painful part, he'd heard. It was what the venom did to your body — how it poisoned your blood and rotted your flesh and then finally stopped your heart.

And there was no cure for a rattlesnake bite. If you were lucky, the doctor could chop off the part of your body the snake bit. But most people died. Last year a girl from his school was bitten while she was running barefoot in the grass. Lucky for her, the snake was just a baby. The little girl only lost a toe.

John shuddered. What was he thinking? He wasn't tough like Rex and the guys. He was just a city kid.

"John," Ma said, putting down her spoon. "Are you feeling all right?"

"You're looking a little green, son," Pa added.

"Oh, no! Johnny's turning into a frog!" Franny said in horror.

Ma had been reading Franny a fairy tale about a witch who turned a prince into a frog.

"That's just a saying, Fran," Ma said. "When a person looks green, it means they feel sick to their stomach."

"Oh, no!" Franny exclaimed. "Johnny's going to throw up!"

"I'm fine," John fibbed, sitting up straighter and digging his fork into his pie.

If he wasn't careful, Ma was going to make him gulp down one of her disgusting medicines. The closest doctor was twenty miles from here — a two-day journey in their rickety wagon. So Ma had a shelf of home remedies — potions and oils and syrups she bought at the general store. Her favorite for upset stomachs was Brown's Bitters. It tasted like a skunk had died in the bottle.

"I feel all right," John said, forcing down a bite of his pie.

"Should be a good day for fishing," Pa said.

"Catch us a big one!" Ma said, rubbing her hands together. "I'll cook it for supper."

John pictured a big fat rattlesnake cooking in Ma's stewpot.

"Yum!" Franny chirped.

John stood up. If he didn't leave now, he'd puke for sure.

John grabbed his cap and said good-bye.

CHAPTER 5

The meeting place was a pond near the creek. John got there first, so he sat at the water's edge to wait. The air was cool, but the sun warmed his back. The water was like a mirror, and it matched the bright blue sky. As usual, the only sound was the moaning wind and the whooshing of the grass.

John's eyes caught something sparkling in the dirt. He dug it out with his thumb. It was an arrowhead, a perfect, flat triangle made of dark metal.

John found arrowheads all the time around here. They belonged to Sioux Indian people who used to live on this land. Probably a Sioux hunter shot this arrow at a buffalo.

Miss Ruell said that there used to be thousands of Sioux people here. They lived in villages and moved across the land with the seasons. In the fall they hunted the buffalo that roamed all over the prairie in giant herds.

John had never met any Sioux people. That's because the American government had made them all leave here. The buffalo were gone, too. Every last one. The giant herds trampled crops and got in the way of building the railroad. So soldiers and settlers shot them all.

John held the arrowhead in his hand. He wondered who it had belonged to. Maybe it was a Sioux boy, a kid like him, hunting with his father like John hunted with Pa. Maybe that kid had a sister like Franny. He could have sat right here, in this exact spot.

Where was that boy now?

John could have wondered about this all day. But just then he heard voices. It was the guys, calling his name. Rex, Peter, and Sven rushed toward him, their snake-killing weapons clutched in their hands. Rex gripped an ax, Peter had a hoe. Sven had a big stick resting on each of his beefy shoulders. He handed one to John.

Peter proudly held up a little canvas bag.

"Three dead mice," he said. "Snake bait."

They set out for the creek, walking side by side, shoulders bumping. From the way the guys were grinning and bouncing with excitement, you'd have thought they were heading to a picnic. John's worries and heavy thoughts soon fell away. The guys chattered nonstop about everything from baseball to girls to whether Miss Ruell would ever get married.

"No way," Peter insisted. "She's twenty-five — way too old."

"And too mean," Sven said.

"What about the cowboy?" Rex asked.

They'd all heard the rumor: that Miss Ruell was engaged to a cowboy.

"I don't believe it," Peter said, shaking his head. None of them liked Miss Ruell. But Peter had a grudge because he got in trouble the most. He couldn't make it through the day without burping out loud or turning his eyelids inside out to make the girls scream.

"I heard that cowboy is in Montana," Sven said. "Building them a house."

"He's probably hiding out there," Peter said. "She's scarier than a grizzly bear!"

"I didn't know grizzly bears wore glasses," Sven laughed.

Peter curled his fingers into circles to make pretend glasses.

"Learn this poem or I will eat you!" he growled.

They all cracked up, including John.

He was glad he wasn't the only one who hated those boring poems.

They kept up their chattering and joking until

they got to the creek. The water was deep and running fast from a big rainstorm the night before.

Suddenly, Rex shopped short.

"That's it," he said quietly. "King Rattler's den."

He pointed to a big rock with a hole underneath.

They all went quiet.

"Look!" Sven whispered.

There was a long, wide groove in the dirt, like a track left by a fat wagon wheel.

Except no one could ever drive a wagon over here.

It was a snake track — left by a huge snake.

It looked fresh.

CHAPTER 6

"Set the bait," Rex said to Peter.

Peter walked up quickly and dropped the dead mice in front of the hole. Then he dashed back. Peter might be a clown. But he was a brave clown.

"Okay," Rex said in a steely voice. "Now we wait. You know what to do."

All week at recess they'd worked out their plan, huddling together like spies while the girls jumped rope and the younger kids played Red Rover.

They figured they'd wait for King Rattler to

poke his head out of his hole. Then they'd rush forward for the attack. Rex would chop the snake's head off with his ax. Peter would hack away with his hoe. Sven and John would stand by to smack it with their sticks.

When it was over, Rex would get to cut off the rattle. That was only fair, since he'd found King Rattler's den and this whole mission was his idea.

They chose a spot a few feet from the hole. They sat in the dirt, with their backs to the creek. John tried not to think about the sound an ax would make when it chopped through the neck of a huge snake.

He wondered what it would do when its head was hacked off. Was it like a chicken, whose body kept moving, even without a head? Would its jaws keep snapping open and shut, fangs shooting out venom? He hoped the guys didn't notice.

They were quiet for a while, but Peter couldn't keep his jaw shut for long. Rex kept shushing him, but it was no use. Soon enough, they were all jabbering again.

They bickered about which candy at the general store was the best, and decided it was a tie between licorice and peppermint sticks.

They talked about the girls at school. The guys all liked Annie, who had curly hair and very white teeth. John liked Myra, who had a loud laugh and was helping Franny learn to jump rope. But he kept that information to himself.

The wind turned colder. None of them were wearing coats, and soon they were rubbing their arms to keep warm.

"My pa says it's going to be a bad winter," Rex told them. "He says blizzards are going to start early."

"How does he know?" John asked, hoping it wasn't such a dumb question.

"Birds have already gone south," Rex said, squinting up at the sky. "Animals know things we don't."

Sven and Peter nodded in agreement.

John wondered how any winter could be more miserable than last year's. He shivered just thinking about the bone-chilling cold. The first blizzard had struck in October. John and Pa were heading home from town when the sky turned dark. The snow started swirling so thick they couldn't see an inch in front of their faces. Luckily their ox, Shadow, stayed on the path and got them home before they were frozen solid.

"At least in winter, there are no grasshoppers," Peter said.

Sven groaned.

"Nothing worse than grasshoppers," added Rex.

John smiled a little because he was sure they were joking. Nobody could be afraid of a little grasshopper. They didn't even sting.

"You never heard about the grasshopper attacks?" Rex asked.

John studied Rex's face, and realized he wasn't joking.

And then, leaning in close, the guys told John the story.

CHAPTER 7

"It happened three years ago, in August." Rex began. "A cloud appeared in the sky from the west."

"It looked like a thunderstorm was coming," Sven said.

"But the cloud looked weird, all shiny," Peter added.

"It got closer and closer," Rex said. "There was this strange sound . . ."

Peter started to click his tongue really fast.

"That whole cloud was made of grasshoppers," Sven said. "There were millions."

"Billions," Rex corrected. "The cloud was ten miles wide."

"And then they all dropped out of the sky," Sven said.

Suddenly the guys all started talking at once, their voices getting louder and louder, their words all swarming together.

The grasshoppers were an inch long.

They have huge eyes that bug out.

They were everywhere!

They'd cover your whole body.

They'd crawl up your pants and down your shirt . . .

And into your ears and up your nose.

John squirmed as he listened. He felt as if hundreds of tiny feet were skittering across his flesh.

"The ground was totally covered with grasshoppers," Peter said.

"They'd crunch when you stepped on them," said Rex. "My boots were covered with grasshopper guts."

John felt queasy.

"And then they ate all the wheat," Rex said.

"*All* the wheat?" John asked.

The guys nodded.

"That's why they came — for the wheat," Rex said. "In just a couple of days they attacked every farm in Prairie Creek. We lost almost all of ours — twenty acres."

"Us, too," Sven said.

"We lost every stalk of wheat," Peter added.

People tried everything to get rid of them. They set fires, shot guns, dumped water onto the wheat stalks. The grasshoppers stuck to the wheat like glue.

The attack lasted a week, until practically every stalk of wheat was chewed down to stubble. The grasshoppers devoured vegetable gardens, too.

"We put blankets over the garden," Rex said. "But the grasshoppers ate the blankets."

John listened in shock. "Then what happened?" he asked.

"They laid their eggs and died."

"We got lucky. We had a cold September, and the freezing cold killed the eggs. Otherwise, they would have hatched, and come back the next year."

That's what had happened in Minnesota.

"The grasshoppers attacked four years in a row," Rex went on.

"Why haven't they come back here?" John asked.

The guys all shook their heads and shrugged.

Then Peter leaned forward. "I got it," he said. "Maybe Miss Ruell scared them away."

They busted out in honks and snorts.

But then they all went quiet again.

"What did people do without their wheat?" John asked.

Growing and selling wheat was the only way to make money here, unless your pa owned a store or worked for the railroad. John couldn't imagine what Ma and Pa would have done if grasshoppers had eaten their wheat crop. They'd have no money to buy coal to keep warm, for clothes, for supplies.

"It was bad," Peter said. "Lots of families left Dakota after that."

"People that stayed helped each other," Rex said. "So we all made it through."

But suddenly Peter's mouth dropped open. His eyes practically popped out of his head.

A chilling sound filled the air.

Shkshkshkshkshkshk

And that's when John saw it, the most massive rattlesnake he'd ever seen — or imagined.

There could be no doubt: It was King Rattler.

He wasn't in his hole. He was just ahead, on the bank of the creek.

And he was coming right for them.

CHAPTER 8

John and the guys all scrambled to their feet. John's heart pounded through his chest.

But none of the guys ran. Somehow, John kept his boots glued to the ground. He stared in horror as the giant snake coiled its body. It was like a thick rope tying itself into a knot. John could see its muscles rippling under its scaly skin. Its head lifted higher and higher as its body coiled more tightly. Soon it was almost as high as their chests. Its forked tongue was flickering in and out, like a candle flame in the wind.

It seemed like a beast from one of Franny's

fairy stories — a fire-breathing dragon, a monster from a dark, dripping cave. It was thicker than John's leg. From its nose to its tail, it had to be taller than Pa — six feet at least. Its skin was dull gold, and covered with black and white triangles. Its rattle was huge, with at least twenty bands — one for every year it had been alive, John had heard. This was an old snake.

Shkshkshkshkshkshkshk

"Don't move," Rex whispered.

It was getting ready to strike, John knew. That's what a rattler does. It coils itself so it can spring forward when it attacks. A rattler that big could leap forward at least six feet, maybe more. These thoughts raced around and around in John's mind, like water spinning in a whirlpool.

There was no way they could kill this snake! Maybe they could have if they had caught it when its head was just peeping out of its hole. But not like this. They'd need a cannon, or an army of soldiers firing rifles. Their stupid snake-killing weapons were useless now. This snake had more than enough venom to kill them all!

41

But the guys weren't ready to surrender.

Rex was standing there, his ax gripped tight in his hand.

Peter held his hoe, ready to strike.

Sven had his stick high in the air.

John felt frozen.

King Rattler was looking directly at *him*. Its deathly yellow eyes glowed. Its mouth opened

wide. Needlelike white fangs glistened inside its sickly pink mouth.

Hissssssssssssss

John's entire body started to shake.

He took a step back, not realizing he was right at the edge of the creek. His foot slipped, and suddenly he was slipping down the bank.

He tumbled backward, landing in the water with a freezing splash. He barely had a chance to take a breath as the churning water grabbed hold of him and sent him rushing downstream.

John couldn't swim — nobody he knew could swim. The water twisted and turned him, scraping him against the rocks as he was carried along. Water gushed into his mouth and up his nose.

He tried to grab hold of rocks and sticks. Anything to slow himself down. But it was no use.

John wasn't going to be killed by a rattlesnake.

He was going to drown!

CHAPTER 9

Finally the water pushed John close enough to the creek bank that he could grab hold of a thorny bush. The prickers tore up his fingers. But John held on tight, and managed to pull himself out of the churning water.

He clawed his way up the bank and sat there in the mud, coughing and wheezing as he tried to catch his breath.

Where were the guys? What had happened to them?

They must think he'd run off, like a scared little rabbit!

The guys would never let him forget this.

He heard footsteps, and voices calling his name. And the guys came bursting out of the bushes, rushing toward him, surrounding him.

John braced himself.

"Are you all right?"

"We lost you!"

"We thought you were a goner!"

They weren't mad at John. They were worried about him!

John forgot his thorn-bitten fingers, and his freezing, mud-soaked clothes. He scrambled to his feet and rushed toward them.

"Did you kill King Rattler?" he asked.

The boys eyed each other. Rex slumped a little. "No. He went into his hole."

And then Peter blurted out, "I was so scared I wet my pants!"

John looked down, and sure enough, there was a big wet stain on Peter's trousers.

Rex frowned at Peter, just like Miss Ruell did when Peter let out a big belch in the middle of a grammar lesson.

But then Rex cracked a smile. And all at once they exploded into laughter, including John.

He laughed at Peter's soaked pants. But also in amazement about what they'd done — they'd faced down King Rattler, the fiercest snake in Dakota!

When they finally calmed down and wiped away their laughing tears, Rex got serious again.

"It was a bad plan," he admitted. "I should have known he wouldn't be in his hole during the day."

"Don't worry," Sven said, putting a comforting hand on Rex's shoulder. "Now we know where he lives. We can come back and get him next Sunday."

"Nah," Rex said. "It's getting too cold. He's going to be hibernating soon. We'll have to wait until spring."

John tried not to show how relieved he felt.

Peter shouted out, "We'll be back for you, King Rattler!"

He waved his empty mouse sack like a flag.

Sven and Rex pumped their fists and stabbed at the sky with their weapons.

They bellowed and hooted. John cheered along with them. He felt like he was at a White Stockings game.

They ran together to the pond and stopped for a few minutes to catch their breath. Then it was finally time to say good-bye and go their separate ways back to their farms.

John walked through the grass toward home. He was shivering in his wet clothes, but he barely noticed. He kept chuckling to himself as he thought of Peter.

John was about a mile from home when he spotted the dark cloud rushing in from the northwest. During his time in Dakota, John had learned to recognize the different kinds of clouds that appeared in the sky. This one was steel gray, and rimmed with white.

John's heart pounded. It was a blizzard cloud.

But how could there be a blizzard coming? It wasn't even October yet!

John remembered Rex's father's prediction of a bad winter, and the fact that the birds had left early. And now John wished he was a bird so he could fly home.

The wind whipped the grasses back and forth. An icy chill filled the air. John shivered in his wet clothes.

He broke into a run, pushing aside the blades of grass. He had to get back to his farm before the snow started to pour down. One of the first things he'd learned in Dakota was to never be outside in a blizzard.

Last year a farmer in Prairie Creek died in a blizzard. He'd been in his barn when it hit, and he tried to get back to his house. It was just twenty feet away. But the snow was so thick in the air that he couldn't find his way. He wandered around in circles until he finally couldn't take another step. His body wasn't found until the spring, when the snow melted.

John ran faster and faster, peering over his shoulder at the looming cloud.

Would he make it home in time?

CHAPTER 10

John was just steps from the soddy when the sky broke open and snow started to pour from the sky. Ma and Pa were standing at the front door, waving him in.

"I was about to come looking for you!" Pa said, pulling John inside and slamming the door.

Ma grabbed a quilt and wrapped it around him.

"I saw the cloud coming," John said, breathing hard and pulling the blanket tight. "I ran the whole way back."

"Who ever heard of a blizzard in September?" Ma fretted.

John told them what Rex had said, that the birds had all flown south early.

Pa frowned. "Those birds could have warned us," he said.

"Daddy, birds don't talk," Franny said, barely looking up from her storybook.

Franny was still too young to understand what a disaster it could be to have a snowstorm so early.

When they'd lived in Chicago, there were stores where they could buy food, no matter what the weather. But here almost everything they ate came from the land. Ma grew their vegetables. They got their milk from Princess the cow and their eggs from their chickens. The creek was loaded with fish. If Ma wanted rabbit or squirrel or goose for her stew, she'd send John or Pa out to shoot one.

But nothing grew when the prairie was covered with ice and snow. The animals disappeared underground. The chickens wouldn't lay eggs, and Princess's milk would dry up. It wasn't until late April that the prairie started to sprout back to life.

And so if they wanted to eat during the frozen months, they had to fill their cellar with food *before* the first big snows.

Ma had been making pickles and jams all summer, and lining up the jars in their little cellar. She had dozens of eggs tucked away in their salty beds. But they still had to harvest the potatoes and turnips, which grew underground.

If this blizzard kept up and the ground froze, those potatoes and turnips would rot. So would the pumpkins and squash still ripening on their vines. They wouldn't have enough to eat this winter.

John stood nervously at the window with Ma and Pa, watching as the snow turned the prairie white. Suddenly Pa pointed into the distance.

"Look!" he exclaimed. "Those clouds are breaking up."

John and Ma followed Pa's finger into the distance. Sure enough, the sky was brightening. The snow slowed, and then finally stopped.

By supper the snow had melted, and the wet prairie grasses sparkled like glass in the setting sun.

"I guess winter changed its mind," Ma said.

"I think it was sending us a message," said Pa. "We'd better get to work."

They started before dawn the next morning. John got out of bed and put on his patched overalls, not his school trousers. He knew he and Franny would be staying home for weeks, and wouldn't go back to school until the work was finished.

Franny helped Ma dig up the potatoes and turnips. John and Pa plowed over the soil in the wheat field so it would ready for planting in the spring. They patched up the soddy roof and filled in the cracks in the dirt walls.

The hardest job was making haystacks. They had to be built just right — tall and tightly packed and rounded at the top — or the hay would rot. That hay would keep Shadow's and

Princess's bellies full over the winter, when there was no grass to munch on.

They worked for weeks. It wasn't until the end of October that the cellar was packed full. The soddy was finally snug. The fields were plowed.

They were ready for winter — as ready as they could ever be.

CHAPTER 11

John clutched Franny's hand tight as they walked along the old wagon trail. It was a cold and dreary October morning and they were finally heading back to school.

John's mind swirled with nervous thoughts. What if the guys had forgotten all about him? What if they ignored him like before?

But just as the school came into view, John heard voices.

"There he is!"

"He's back!"

Rex, Peter, and Sven came barreling over to

him. They grabbed his arm and slapped his back so hard he almost fell to the dirt.

But of course John didn't mind.

For the first time since he left Chicago, John actually looked forward to going to school.

At lunchtime he and the guys would squeeze together around one desk. They'd divvy up whatever food they'd brought from home. Sven's mother baked the best bread, the dark Swedish kind that tasted smoky and sweet. Peter's made the most delicious pies. John's favorite was made from the sour chokecherries that grew wild on the prairie. Rex got the same lunch every day: two potatoes, roasted in their skins. He didn't complain, though. He said that on cold days he carried one hot potato in each pocket, to keep his hands warm.

John learned more about the guys and how their families had come to Dakota.

Rex's family came from Texas, and traveled to Dakota before their town, Prairie Creek, even had a name. Rex didn't remember the month-long journey in a covered wagon. But he knew

CANADA

DAKOTA
TERRITORY

MT
Terr.

Wyoming
Territory

Colorado

the whole family almost drowned when they were bringing their wagon across the Colorado River.

Sven came from the farthest away — Sweden. The trip took almost six months by ship, train, and wagon. The worst part was the two-month voyage across the Atlantic in a leaky steamship crawling with mice. Sven spent most of the trip puking over the side.

But it was Peter's story that hit John the hardest. His family came five years ago, from Minnesota. Crossing into Dakota, they ran into a thunderstorm. The mules pulling their wagon got spooked and took off. The wagon nearly flipped over. And Peter's little brother, William, flew out. He landed on some rocks and died within the hour.

"My ma didn't talk for six months after that," Peter said softly.

John swallowed hard, and he noticed Rex and Sven did, too.

None of them said anything more, but they all inched a little closer to Peter.

John didn't think he had any important stories to share. He'd never crossed a stormy ocean or a raging river.

But one bright day at recess, the guys started asking John about Chicago. It turned out none of them had ever been to a big city. And they were dying to hear all about skyscrapers and restaurants and the electric lights that lit up the streets at night.

"Lots of murderers live there, right?" Peter asked.

"Maybe," John said. "I never met one, though."

The guys seemed a little disappointed.

"I heard there are rats as big as cats," Sven said.

"There are," John said, and he told how once he woke up and found one sitting right on his bed.

"What did you do?" Rex asked.

John shrugged. "Just shooed it away."

The guys fell over in laughing horror.

You'd have thought John had fought off a dragon.

"I hate rats," Rex said with a shudder. John found it amazing — this was a kid who'd stared down a monster snake, and a plain old rat gave him the willies!

But John understood. To the guys, Chicago was a strange land, one filled with danger and mystery. Like Dakota was to John.

"What's the weather like there?" Sven asked.

John shrugged. "It gets hot in the summer, and cold in the winter," he said. "But nothing like here."

The guys nodded.

Peter looked up at the sunny sky.

"I'm thinking that maybe winter's not going to be so bad," he said. "It's been warm all week."

"Remember, the birds left early," Sven said.

"The birds could be wrong," Peter said.

They all looked at Rex, who was polishing off his second potato.

Rex just shook his head.

"The birds are never wrong."

CHAPTER 12

The first big blizzard hit the very next week, a howling storm that came in the night and lasted for three days. The weather cleared up until early November, and then it snowed on and off for most of the next two months.

A Christmas Day ice storm left icicles hanging off the soddy roof, and all the way to the ground. Franny licked one and got her tongue stuck. Ma had to melt some of the icicle with warm water so poor Franny's tongue wouldn't tear in half.

But it turned out that winter was just getting started.

On January 5, John woke up shivering. The inside of the soddy walls shimmered with white frost. His teeth chattered so hard he was afraid they'd shatter.

Pa checked the thermometer outside their front door.

"Minus twenty," he announced with a *brrrrrrr*.

Ma fed more coal into the stove, but it didn't do much good. When it got this cold outside, even the thick dirt walls of the soddy couldn't keep the warm air from seeping out.

Of course it was too cold for school. Nobody could go out in this weather. John wished he could stay in bed, wrapped tight in his quilt. But Shadow and Princess needed breakfast. He bundled up in his heavy woolen coat and scarf and mittens and stepped outside.

The cold seemed to reach into his lungs and freeze his breath. His eyes watered and the tears froze to his cheeks. He rushed into the barn and warmed himself up by huddling next to Shadow.

He tried to milk Princess, but only a few

squirts came out. And the milk froze before it even hit the bucket.

As he came out of the barn, he saw Pa standing in front of one of their haystacks. It looked like someone — or something — had chewed right through its center.

"What happened?" John asked.

"Some animal must have slept there last night," Pa said.

John noticed little paw prints leading to and from the stack.

"Looks like it was a fox," Pa said.

"He hid in a haystack?" John asked.

"Sure," Pa said. "The walls are good and thick, keeps the cold out."

John helped Pa fix the haystack. By the time he came in for breakfast, his face was completely numb. Icicles hung from his eyelashes. It took two mugs of Ma's tea to warm him up again.

For a solid week, they couldn't leave the soddy except to feed the animals and to get water. They couldn't even use the outhouse. Ma put up a curtain in the corner, and they used a bucket.

As the days dragged by, John started to feel like a pickle trapped in a jar — a cold and very smelly jar.

But on the morning of January 12, Franny shook John awake.

"It's summer!" she announced.

"Not quite," Pa laughed. "But it warmed up. It's almost thirty degrees!"

And after the bone-cracking cold of the last week, it did feel practically like summer. John had only one thought: They would be able to go to school.

John rushed through his chores and gobbled up his porridge, and he and Franny flew out the door.

Ma called after them from the doorway.

"Wait! Your mittens and scarves!"

"Don't need them, Ma!" John hollered back.

"It's summer, Ma, remember?" Franny laughed.

As she and John walked, Franny looked up at the sky.

"Look," she said. "It looks like a fairy tale."

The sky did look different, pale blue and streaked with gold.

John had never seen anything like it.

CHAPTER 13

After seven days of being cooped up because of the cold, the kids at school acted like bank robbers who'd escaped from jail. Nobody wanted to sit still. And to their surprise, Miss Ruell cut their grammar lesson short.

"I wouldn't mind a little fresh air," she said.

The schoolhouse erupted in cheers.

John and the guys leapt out of their seats.

Kids poured outside, most without their coats and wraps. Franny ran off to play hide-and-seek with her friends.

John and the guys stayed in front. The hard-packed snow was slick, like an ice rink. They slid around, racing each other and spinning until they were too dizzy to stand. John was sliding across when someone came up right next to him.

Myra!

"Race you," she said, smiling as she whooshed by. Her flowered dress billowed behind her like a sail.

John's heart somersaulted inside his chest. He tried to catch up with her, but she ran off giggling with Annie. John wondered if the guys had seen that. He looked around and realized they weren't skating anymore. They were on the schoolhouse steps.

John went over. They all looked uneasy. Rex was peering into the sky to the north of them.

"What's wrong?" John asked.

"See that?" Rex said.

John followed Rex's gaze.

And that's when John saw it in the distance, a gray shadow in the sky. At first he thought he was imagining it, that the blinding brightness of the day was making his eyes play tricks.

But no. Rex was right. There was something in the sky, something big and dark. And it was getting bigger by the second. It was coming this way, and moving very fast.

Rex's mouth fell open. "What the . . ."

They all stood and watched as the shadow in the distance took shape. With each second, it got bigger and darker. It was a cloud of some kind, dirty gray and billowing, and stretching out across the land.

The temperature was dropping, fast. John was shivering, not just because of the cold. He didn't know what he was looking at. He just knew it was bad.

The schoolyard went quiet. Kids stopped sliding in the snow. All eyes were on the churning cloud.

"That's a huge storm," Rex said. "I've never seen anything like it."

A low rumbling rose up. The ground shook.

And now Miss Ruell was clanging the bell.

"Children! Come inside now! Hurry!"

The day seemed to turn to night. And then came an earsplitting roar. It sounded like a train was speeding right by them. But of course there was no train anywhere near here.

It was the sound of a monster blizzard, closing in.

Kids rushed into the schoolhouse. John was swept up the stairs in the wave of panicked bodies. Suddenly he was inside. The schoolhouse door banged shut.

And then,

ROOOOOOAAAAR!

CHAPTER 14

The entire building shook. A window shattered, and snow and ice exploded into the schoolhouse. But John hardly noticed. He barely heard the screeching wind or the cries of the little kids. He was looking all around.

Where was Franny?

It was very dark inside the schoolhouse. Miss Ruell struggled to light a lantern. But John could see well enough to know that Franny wasn't there.

A crack of fear almost knocked him off his feet.

She'd been playing hide-and-seek. She'd probably found some perfect hiding spot off in a corner of the schoolyard. And when everyone ran inside, she'd been left behind.

How had John let that happen? How could he have forgotten his sister?

John rushed to the door and flung it open. A vicious blast of wind and snow nearly knocked him down. He clung to the doorframe to keep his balance.

"Franny!" he cried.

Miss Ruell called to him.

"John! No!"

But John couldn't wait. Franny was out there!

The storm's icy hooks seemed to snatch him from the doorway. The wind roared in his ears and yanked him down the stairs. It threw him onto the ground. Ice and snow lashed his face. He gasped for breath as the freezing air shocked his lungs.

John grabbed the stair railing and struggled to his feet. He pushed himself forward, staggering into the frozen darkness that had swallowed the schoolyard.

"Franny!" he cried.

ROOOOARRR! the storm screamed back.

He looked around, but it was impossible to see. The snow gushed down from the sky and churned in the wind. Ground-up ice flew into John's eyes, coating his lashes and lids. With each blink, the ice scraped painfully against his eyeballs.

But even worse was the furious wind, which slashed at him from every direction. John felt as if he was locked in a cage with a pack of wild beasts, all trying to tear him to bits.

He thought of that farmer who'd died in last year's blizzard. It hadn't really made sense to John, how a strong man could get lost and freeze to death, just a few yards from his house. But now, as John staggered blindly along, spinning in the wind, he understood all too well.

Crushed bits of snow sifted down his collar and blew up his sleeves and trouser legs. Soon, every inch of his skin was crusted with ice. The cold seeped through his flesh and muscles, and stabbed into his bones.

John was shivering so hard his bones felt as if they would crack apart.

A gust of wind smashed against him. He fell back, into the snow. And now he couldn't stand up. The wind pressed down on him, like a giant boot crushing him into the ground. Ice was filling his nose, making it harder and harder to breathe.

A feeling of terror came over John. He had never felt so tiny, and so helpless.

He'd made a terrible mistake, he realized.

There was no way he would be able to find Franny in this blizzard.

He was going to freeze to death.

CHAPTER 15

John mustered the last of his strength and screamed out at the top of his lungs.

"Franny!"

The blizzard screamed back.

But then another voice punched through the blizzard's howl.

"John!"

It wasn't Franny.

It was Miss Ruell. Her voice was muffled by the wind. But he thought she was somewhere very close.

And then a hand clamped onto his arm.

74

Miss Ruell had found him!

She gripped his arm tighter and managed to pull him up.

John was so freezing cold that his body wasn't working right. He couldn't feel his feet. He kept stumbling and falling to his knees.

Luckily, Miss Ruell was stronger than she looked. She wrapped her arm around John's waist. And she practically dragged him through the rising snowdrifts and up the steps to the schoolhouse door. The next thing John knew, he was inside.

He collapsed onto the floor.

He couldn't see through his frozen eyes. But he felt people surrounding him. Hands swept snow from his head. Gentle fingers brushed ice from his face. A blanket came around his shoulders. John would have died of embarrassment if he wasn't practically frozen to death.

And then someone hugged him. John smelled apples and soap.

Could it be? Was he dreaming?

"Franny?"

Hot tears welled up in John's eyes, melting the ice that crusted his lashes and lids. He stared at his sister's face.

He had never in his life felt so relieved.

"Why did you go outside!" she cried.

"I thought you were lost!" John stuttered through his chattering teeth. "I was looking for you!"

"I snuck inside and was here hiding under Miss Ruell's desk, for the game."

No wonder John didn't see her.

"Help John up and let's get him closer to the stove," Miss Ruell said.

Peter, Rex, and Sven all lifted John to his feet and practically carried him across the room. Myra brought over a chair so he could sit. The guys hovered around him. Franny glued herself to John's side.

But Miss Ruell shooed everyone away.

"Let him get warm," she said.

Myra took Franny by the hand, and the guys moved away.

Miss Ruell was still covered with snow. She was untying a rope that was knotted around her waist. John realized she must have tied the other end to something in the schoolhouse. That's how she had made sure she would be able to find her way back inside.

How smart of Miss Ruell. And brave.

She must think he was a fool, to run outside in the blizzard. She must hate him more than ever.

John took a breath.

"I'm sorry, ma'am," he said.

His teacher looked at him with surprise.

She wasn't wearing her glasses. Her bun had come loose. Brown curls hung around her face.

She didn't look scary.

"You thought your sister was out there," she said. "What you did was brave."

Their eyes locked together for a moment. A gentle smile flickered across his teacher's face. She patted John's arm before she walked back to her desk.

Maybe it was the fire in the stove. But suddenly, John felt warmer.

The wind screamed louder. The schoolhouse walls shuddered, and the windows rattled. But Miss Ruell, her hair back in its bun, was steely and calm.

She gave all the older kids jobs. When John was warmed up again, he helped the guys sweep away the snow that was sifting under the door and through the cracks in the walls. Myra and Annie kept watch over the little kids and soon had them playing Simon Says. Moving around helped them stay warm.

John kept his eye on Franny. But now he couldn't stop thinking about Ma and Pa. What if Pa had been out in the field when the blizzard hit? What if Ma had been in the barn?

It was very cold in the schoolhouse, even with Miss Ruell feeding extra coal into the roaring fire in the stove. John kept looking at the coal bin. There was barely enough coal to last a few hours more. What would happen when all the coal was gone?

They'd have to burn the books, and then the desks.

And after that?

John tried not to think about it.

CHAPTER 16

Suddenly, the schoolhouse door flew open with a loud bang. An icy blast of freezing air and snow exploded into the room.

The wind had ripped off the door!

But no. It wasn't the wind.

Three men stumbled into the schoolhouse. One of them wrestled the door closed again. The men stood there, breathing hard. They were so caked with snow and ice they looked like walking snowmen.

Myra went running over.

"Papa!" she said, ignoring the snow that covered him and throwing her arms around him.

The other men were Mr. Johnson and Mr. Lowry, who owned stores in town.

"We've got three sleds outside," Myra's father said, his voice rising over the wind. "Plenty of room for everyone. Blankets, too. We're going to get you into town, to the hotel. We can wait out the blizzard there and then get everyone home when the storm is over."

Cheers rang out.

They'd been rescued!

Peter held up his broom and hooted.

Miss Ruell closed her eyes, looked up, and whispered something to herself. And then she clapped her hands and called the class to order.

"Everyone get their coats and wraps and line up."

"Let's be quick," said Myra's father. "Storm's getting worse. The horses are freezing."

Miss Ruell divided the children into three groups. She would ride in the biggest sled in the front, with the six youngest children.

Myra and Annie would take charge of three younger girls and go with Mr. Johnson in the second sled.

John and the guys would be in the third sled with Mr. Lowry.

John didn't want to be away from Franny. But there was no way he could argue. And he knew Miss Ruell would keep her safe.

Myra's father flung open the door, and they faced the brutal cold. It was more freezing now than it had been when John was stuck outside. The snow poured down harder. It was like standing under a waterfall made of snow and ice. Within seconds they were all covered.

John held Franny's hand tight as they pushed through the wild, frozen swirl. There were lanterns on each sled. The lanterns cast a ghostly yellow light, just enough to show the outline of the sleds. Each was a simple wooden wagon mounted on metal sled rails, and hitched to a single horse. John felt so sorry for those horses. Their fur wasn't much protection in cold this harsh. He wondered how long they'd be able to stand it.

John lifted Franny into the first wagon and made sure she was wrapped in a blanket.

It was useless to try to talk over the screaming, hissing wind. He hugged his sister tight and then hurried back to his sled. He climbed up and settled down next to Rex. Mr. Lowry was already in the driver's seat, holding the reins.

John and the guys had one big blanket to share. They put it over their heads, to try to keep the snow and ice out of their faces. But it was useless. The snow was ground up so fine it completely filled the air. The glassy ice raked at his eyeballs, like tiny claws. John sat there, miserable and shivering. But he reminded himself that they were close to town — the trip shouldn't take more than ten minutes. The guys weren't complaining, were they? John had to be tough.

Finally, the first sled started to move, and its yellow glowing lantern light disappeared. The second sled followed. Mr. Lowry was about to snap the reins to get their horse moving. But just then the wind let out a vicious howl. There was a crunch, and a hunk of the schoolhouse roof came flying through the air. It smacked the horse on the back.

The horse reared in terror. The sled rocked and almost tipped over. Mr. Lowry tumbled out onto the ground. The horse took off in panic, dragging the sled — and John and the guys — along with it.

And now they were speeding through the blizzard, out of control.

CHAPTER 17

Rex crawled forward and tried to grab hold of the reins. But it was hopeless. The horse was running so fast the sled was practically off the ground. It rocked back and forth like a tiny boat on a storm-tossed ocean. Every time the sled hit a bump, the wood cracked and groaned.

"We have to jump!" Rex screamed.

He was right. Any moment the sled was going to break apart. They could be trampled under the horse's hooves or crushed by the sled.

"Go!" Rex cried.

Heart hammering, John struggled to his feet.

He closed his eyes, held his breath, and threw himself off the side.

He landed hard, and rolled away as the metal sled rail sliced by him, inches from his head. John lay there, panting.

Finally, he sat up. To his relief, Sven was right next to him. And Rex and Peter were behind. They all crawled closer to each other and sat in a huddle.

Nobody had gotten hurt from the jump off the sled. But they were all shivering — hard. John's hands and feet were completely numb. They couldn't last out here for much longer.

Rex was looking all around.

"We're near the Ricker farm," he shouted.

The Rickers had a real wooden house, with three rooms.

"I'm pretty sure the house is right over there," Rex shouted.

"Where?" Sven shouted back.

Rex looked around.

"Close!"

John's heart sank.

Close.

That word meant nothing in a blizzard like this. The schoolhouse had been just a few feet away while John was staggering around the schoolyard. If Miss Ruell hadn't come to rescue him, he'd be a frozen corpse by now, buried in the snow.

It would be almost impossible to find the Ricker house. It might as well be on the moon.

But they had two choices: Get moving or freeze to death right here. So when Rex shouted, "Come on!" they all struggled to their feet and followed.

They staggered through the wall of slashing snow and ice. The wind's nonstop scream burrowed through John's skull, deep into his brain. It was taunting John, hissing at him as he tried to push his way forward.

You're weak.

You can't make it.

You're doomed!

That wind was right. John didn't belong out here in Dakota. He'd always known it. And now he'd never escape.

John walked with his head down, crouched over like an old man, pushing himself through the wall of wind and ice and snow. He could make it only a few steps without falling. One of his friends would grab his arms and yank him back up. And then Rex would fall down, or Peter or Sven. And it would be John helping lift them up.

On and on they went. Battered by the maniac wind. Lashed by the ground-glass ice. Falling down. Standing up. Falling down. Standing up.

Colder, colder, colder.

And then came a savage gust. An ice-packed whirl so furious it knocked them all down at once.

And this time, not one of them could stand back up. Not even Rex.

They sat there, sinking deeper into the snow.

John felt the last of his body's warmth seeping out of him, like blood leaking from a deep cut.

That screaming wind was right, John thought. They were doomed.

CHAPTER 18

Precious minutes ticked by, and none of them moved. It was getting colder.

But down here, close to the ground, the wind wasn't quite as strong. The air wasn't as thick with swirling snow. John managed to wipe the frozen snow from his eyes.

Which is why he saw it, the outline of something very big, just a few yards ahead.

"There's the house!" John shouted.

They all lunged forward, crawling desperately through the snowdrifts.

John's heart pounded with excitement.

They'd made it! They'd be safe!

The boys pushed themselves along, fighting their way forward. It wasn't until they were just inches away that they saw that it wasn't the Ricker house.

It was a big haystack.

Peter let out a big sob.

Rex cursed and looked around.

"The house must be this way!" he shouted.

Rex stepped forward, but John grabbed the back of his jacket and pulled him back.

"No!" John shouted.

John might not be a real pioneer like Rex. This was only his second Dakota winter. But he knew this for sure: They'd never find the Ricker house, not in time. They had to get out of this wind and snow. They had to try to get warm.

Inside the haystack.

John remembered the fox that had hidden in their haystack overnight. Didn't Rex say that animals were always right?

John turned to Rex. "We won't make it," he shouted over the wind. "We have to take cover in here."

And now John took the lead.

He punched a hole through the thick crust of snow and ice that covered the haystack. He reached through and grabbed fistfuls of the soft hay to make space. Rex and Peter and Sven were helping him. They worked desperately, jabbing their hands in, pulling out hay.

They all worked together until they had a little cave, big enough for them all to fit. And then they crawled in, lying flat and squeezed together.

It was still freezing cold. John's numb hands and feet felt like blocks of wood. He couldn't stop shivering. But finally the cruel wind couldn't reach them. The ice and snow couldn't tear at their faces. And soon the heat from their bodies started to warm up the small space.

"Don't sleep," Rex said.

John had heard what happened to people who fell asleep in the freezing cold.

They never woke up. That's why freezing to death wasn't the worst way to die, he'd heard. Because you fall asleep before your heart stops.

And so now they fought hard against sleep, just like they'd fought against the wind and snow. They took turns telling stories. They counted to one thousand and then did it again backward. They said prayers. John told them the name of every player on the Chicago White Stockings.

The hours passed. The blizzard raged on. They ran out of stories and got tired of counting. And then Peter started muttering in a strange, rhyming way. And John realized he was reciting one of the long, boring poems Miss Ruell had made them memorize. They all joined him. And then they recited another, and another. They all knew so many.

It turned out that not all of those poems were so boring. Some were about pirates and sailors. One was about the summer, and the words made John feel warmer. There were poems that made no sense, like one about a pig wearing a wig. But it actually made them laugh.

Those poems kept them up for hours more.

But finally, their voices became ragged.

Their words faded away.

John's mind started to drift.

Don't sleep! Don't sleep!

His eyes fluttered.

Don't sleep! Don't sleep!

John's eyes shut.

Don't sleep, don't . . .

John's eyes stayed closed.

Everything got quiet, even the sound of that screaming wind.

Was this ferocious storm finally dying?

Or was John?

CHAPTER 19

ABOUT TWO WEEKS LATER

Newspapers from New York to Seattle printed stories about the deadly blizzard that had struck America's northern prairie.

It was one of the most powerful snowstorms ever to hit America, more like a frozen hurricane than a blizzard. Winds had reached 70 miles an hour. Temperatures had dipped down to minus 40. Cities like St. Paul, Minnesota, and Lincoln, Nebraska, were shut down. Towns were buried. Hundreds were dead.

It was a blizzard so terrible that soon it had a name:

The Children's Blizzard.

Because at least one hundred of the people who died were schoolchildren.

The newspapers were filled with sad and terrible stories about children who became trapped in the frozen, swirling winds.

But there were miracles, too.

Like how one teacher tied her ten students together with a rope and led them to a farmhouse a half mile away from their school. Or the kids who made it through the night in a shelter they built from snow. Or the brothers who huddled in a barn with two pigs that kept them warm.

And the four boys from the tiny town of Prairie Creek, Dakota, who survived the blizzard in a haystack.

John didn't read any of those stories, not at first.

For the first week after the blizzard, he wasn't sure if he was alive or dead. The storm had ended just a few minutes after he and the guys had fallen asleep. They had been in that haystack almost all night.

John was barely breathing when Mr. and Mrs. Ricker carried him and the other boys from the haystack and into the farmhouse. When Ma and Pa got there, later that day, he heard them calling his name. He felt their hands on him.

But he couldn't open his eyes. He couldn't move or speak. He felt locked away, caught in a frozen nightmare.

Most of the time, he thought he was still in the haystack, or curled into a snowdrift. That hissing blizzard scream still echoed in his ears.

It wasn't until a week after the blizzard that John finally opened his eyes. It was the middle of the night, and it took him a long, panicked moment to understand that he wasn't in the haystack. Or in a frozen grave.

He was in the warm soddy, tucked into his bed. Franny was curled up next to him. Pa was dozing in a chair, pulled close. Ma was sitting on John's bed.

"Ma?" John said, in a crackling voice.

The fire in the stove cast a golden glow, and John saw the tears in Ma's eyes as she smiled down at him.

And that was the moment when, for John, the terrifying blizzard at last came to an end.

CHAPTER 20

ABOUT THREE MONTHS LATER
SUNDAY, APRIL 29, 1888
PRAIRIE CREEK, DAKOTA TERRITORY
AFTERNOON

The snow had melted, and the prairie was slowly sprouting back to life. Bright green shoots pushed up through the brown grass. Enormous flocks of geese and ducks flapped across the blue sky.

The winter was over. The birds were back.

John and the guys had returned to school at

the end of March. And now, on this bright and warm day in April, here they were at the creek.

They'd come for King Rattler.

John had brought Pa's rifle this time. Rex clutched his ax, and Sven was ready with his stick. Peter had found a dead rabbit, half-eaten by a fox. That was the bait.

"King Rattler could attack from any direction," Rex reminded them, his voice strong but still raspy from months of coughing. He'd caught a bad case of pneumonia after the blizzard, and looked too skinny and frail.

They were all still healing.

Sven lost two toes from frostbite and was walking with a cane.

Peter had lost a pinky.

"I never liked that finger anyway," he swore.

John's feet had been so badly frostbitten that he nearly lost them — his hands, too. His feet had swelled up like balloons. The skin on his hands and feet turned black, like meat left too long on the fire. The pain was so terrible that he couldn't move. For days he was in bed, soaked in sweat and trying not to cry.

But Ma kept telling him that the pain was good news, that it meant blood was starting to flow again, that his hands and feet were coming back to life. She kept dosing John with Brown's Bitters and gently rubbing his skin with some cream that smelled like rotten apples.

Slowly the black skin peeled away. Underneath was brand-new skin — soft and pink.

"Your feet look like piglets!" Franny had shrieked happily.

John stared at his bright pink feet and realized Franny was right. He started to laugh, and Ma and Pa did, too. And after that, some of the gloom cleared from the soddy.

It helped that people from town kept coming to visit them. They brought food, precious jars of berry jam and baskets of eggs from their cellars. Myra visited and gave John a scarf she had knitted herself. Mr. Lowry came, and told them what happened to him after the horse bolted with the sled. He'd made it back into the schoolhouse and had burned the desks to stay warm through the night.

Miss Ruell stopped by a few times. Of course John had to tell her about those long poems she'd made them memorize, how they helped John and the guys stay awake in the haystack. Miss Ruell flashed a smile, big and bright.

By then, John had heard the big news: Miss Ruell was getting married. She would be leaving Dakota this summer and moving to Montana. John would miss her. He knew the guys would, too. Even Peter.

"I hear she's invited the whole town to the wedding," Rex said now. "It's going to be at the schoolhouse."

"What should we get her for a present?" Sven asked.

They were stumped.

"I know!" Rex said, his eyes lighting up. "King Rattler's rattle!"

They all grinned.

Rex was a genius! Who wouldn't want a huge snake rattle as a wedding gift?

They argued about what food would be best for the wedding: chokeberry pie or molasses cake. They swore they wouldn't wear their itchy church clothes but thought they might have to. They hoped Miss Ruell's man would wear his cowboy hat.

And then there was a rustling sound in the bushes.

"Shhhh!" Rex said.

They all jumped up.

John gripped Pa's gun. Rex raised his ax. Sven held up his cane. Peter looked ready to pounce.

It was time to finally kill King Rattler!

CHAPTER 21

The boys all waited. John's heart pounded.

And then it appeared from the bushes:

An enormous . . .

. . . frog.

It looked at them with its bulging eyes.

"Croak!"

They all cracked up and watched the frog hop away.

And now it was getting late, and time to head home.

"We'll be back for you, King Rattler!" Peter shouted.

They headed back to the pond, shoulders bumping, smiling and joking as they limped along. They said their good-byes and John made his way back toward his farm.

He breathed in the smell of new grass and fresh dirt. Soon he and Pa would be planting their wheat field. If their crop was a good one, they'd have enough money to start building a

real house, made of wood. With two rooms —
practically a castle compared to the soddy.

There would be more work than ever as they
readied their field.

John thought nervously about what the spring
and summer could bring.

Thunderstorms. Hail. Prairie fires. Funnel
clouds. Grasshoppers.

Dakota was a harsh land.

But they were staying here, at least for now.

Ma and Pa had talked about leaving, in those
terrible weeks after the blizzard. John had heard
them whispering softly at night, when they
thought he was asleep. That storm had terrified
his parents. They'd been so desperate to find
John and Franny that Pa had gone out into the
storm.

He'd realized his mistake right away; within
five steps Pa was completely lost in the white
swirl. He stumbled blindly. And then he heard a
bell clanging over the roaring wind. It was Ma,
standing in the doorway, leading him home.

Leave or stay, leave or stay. Ma and Pa

weren't sure what to do. They'd poured every cent — and their hearts — into this farm. And what would they do back in Chicago? Pa had left his job. How would they pay for an apartment? How would they buy food?

They couldn't plant a wheat field in Chicago. Their neighbors in the city had never visited with pies and eggs and jars of jelly. This would be their one and only chance to own a farm.

And so finally, Ma and Pa decided to stay put.

And John was glad. Because how could he leave the guys?

There would be more storms ahead, John knew. But somehow they'd all made it through the blizzard. Whatever was coming, they would face it.

Maybe that's what it meant to be a pioneer.

John was about halfway home when something caught his eye, maybe twenty feet to the side.

It was a snake. A massive snake.

John stopped breathing.

Could it be?

It was King Rattler!

The giant snake was stretched out in the grass. His diamond skin gleamed. His tongue flickered in and out.

Moving very slowly, John lifted Pa's rifle. He took aim at the giant snake.

Imagine what the guys would say when he brought them the rattle!

John put his finger on the trigger.

He steadied himself.

King Rattler didn't move. And lying there, he actually didn't look that fierce. He looked like a very old snake trying to soak up some last rays of sun.

John wondered: How long had that big snake been on this land?

A very long time. Longer than any of them.

Suddenly it seemed wrong to John, that this old snake would be gone.

He lowered the gun and walked quickly away.

They'd have to think of a different present for Miss Ruell.

—

John walked a mile more, his feet aching.

Finally he saw their soddy in the distance. He spotted Ma digging in her garden, getting it ready for spring planting. Franny was dancing around outside. Shadow and Princess grazed on tender green sprouts. Pa was on the roof of the barn, patching up the last of the winter holes. He saw John and waved.

The afternoon sun had turned the brown grass bright gold.

Whoosh.

The warm breeze blew, pushing John along.

Whoosh. It seemed to whisper gently into his ear.

You're home.

MY PRAIRIE JOURNEY

Dear Readers,

Close your eyes and imagine that you live in a tiny dirt house, crammed into one room with your family. You look out the window and all you can see is flat, empty land covered with tall grass. Your closest neighbor is an hour's walk away, through land infested with rattlesnakes. You live in fear of the dark clouds that suddenly appear in the sky, bringing thunderstorms and blizzards and tornados . . . and even billions of grasshoppers.

This was the real life of hundreds of thousands

of people in the late 1800s and early 1900s. They were pioneers. They traveled west to build farms on America's prairie — the vast stretch of flat, grassy land, mostly in North and South Dakota, Montana, Minnesota, Nebraska, and Kansas. Many had been living in cities or towns in the east. Others came from Europe.

They came with dreams of building farms and making better lives.

What they found was hardship. Most pioneers, also known as *homesteaders*, gave up on their farms after just a few years.

The biggest challenge was the weather. Few areas of the world have more extreme weather than parts of the American Midwest, especially in the North. The summers are boiling hot and often bone-dry. Winter temperatures can plunge to minus 30 degrees. Spring brings thunderstorms, with pounding hail and tornadoes. There are also droughts, prairie fires, and dust storms. Grasshopper attacks really happened — for years and years. And of course there were blizzards.

But some people did manage to stay, in spite of all the hardship. With grit and determination and plenty of luck, they built up their farms. They helped create some of the cities and towns that are still there today.

One of those towns is Wessington Springs, South Dakota, in the middle of the state. In 1888, a few hundred families lived in Wessington Springs. When the blizzard struck, seven kids were stranded in their freezing schoolhouse with their young teacher, May Hunt. They all survived the night by hiding in a haystack.

My husband and I wanted to visit the town's small history museum. We had made an appointment to meet the museum's volunteer director, Eileen Woodruff.

Little did we know that some I Survived and *Storyworks* readers would be waiting for us. They had gathered in the town's small library, with Tammy Mettler, the town librarian.

We drank lemonade and ate Rice Krispies treats and talked about the town's history. People shared their own family stories, about relatives who'd built farms, who'd died from rattlesnake bites and withstood grasshopper attacks. In the middle of all of this, a voice called out "Someone needs to call Lorraine."

A call was made. Minutes later, in walked Lorraine Redmann, who has lived in Wessington Springs for most of her long life. She had more stories to share, like that of a man who survived the blizzard huddling in a barn with a pig. "After that," Lorraine said, "you could not say a bad word about a pig when he was near."

Afterward, Eileen took us back to the museum, the Jerauld County Pioneer Museum. (You must visit!) The museum is in a plain brick building that used to be a bank. Inside is a treasure trove of history. There are thousands of objects from the area's past — furniture, old rifles, hunting knives, dishes, and bottles of medicines such as Brown's Bitters. There are also arrowheads, robes, and clothing that belonged to the Sioux and other native peoples who had been living on the land for thousands of years before the settlers arrived.

As I left Wessington Springs, I started to imagine the characters and plot of my I Survived book about the blizzard. I could picture John and his family, his pals at the schoolhouse, and King Rattler.

As my husband and I traveled down the highway, driving a straight line through the Dakota prairie, I felt a special kind of joy. I had made new friends. I felt lucky to have heard their stories. And I couldn't wait to share those stories with you.

Lauren Tarshis

Pioneers standing in front of their sod house, similar to the one that John and his family would have lived in.

QUESTIONS AND ANSWERS ABOUT THE CHILDREN'S BLIZZARD AND LIFE IN 1888

Why was the Children's Blizzard such a dangerous storm?

The blizzard was huge, powerful, and fast-moving. Some scientists have compared it to a hurricane because of its vicious, swirling winds.

But what made this blizzard especially danger-ous is that it struck on such a warm day, when most people were simply not expecting a storm. A few "old-timers" (like Rex's dad) did sense something menacing in the sudden rise in temperature, in the unnaturally warm January day.

But most people were just happy to have a break from the brutal cold that had gripped the prairie the week before. Kids flocked to school. Farmers rushed into their fields to fix fences and took their animals out to get exercise.

People had no warning that the storm was on the way.

Today, weather scientists have high-tech tools for tracking blizzards and other storms. They can predict when and where these dangerous storms will strike. We can check the weather on our computers. Weather alerts buzz on our phones.

In 1888, however, the science of weather forecasting — known as meteorology — was still very new. Scientists didn't really understand weather patterns. And there was no way for people to know what was coming — until that black cloud appeared.

And then it was too late.

Was the Children's Blizzard the deadliest blizzard to strike America?

About 235 people died in the Children's Blizzard. Many were children, which is why the event was especially tragic, and why it is remembered more than any other prairie blizzard in history.

I was surprised to learn that the deadliest blizzard in America struck just two months after the Children's Blizzard, in March 1888. It hit the East Coast, burying cities and towns from Maine down to Washington, DC. New York City got hit especially hard. More than 200 people died in New York City alone.

The Children's Blizzard was likely a more powerful storm than the one that hit the East. But because there were so many more people living in eastern cities, the death toll was higher in the March storm.

New York City after the blizzard of 1888

What was life like in America at the time of the blizzard?

Life was different depending on where in the country you lived, just as in America today. That was even more true back in 1888.

In cities like New York and Chicago, life was becoming more and more modern. Electric lights blazed in the streets. Gleaming steel bridges crossed rivers. There were fancy department stores, baseball stadiums, concert halls, and theaters. Kids went to big schools with hundreds of students. People even had toilets — inside their homes. (That was modern!)

But in America's small towns, life hadn't changed much in a hundred years. There were few roads. Most people were farmers. Kids worked alongside their parents, and went to one-room schools. Toilets were outside, pits dug in the ground.

For people like John and his family, living in tiny towns in the West, life could be especially challenging.

How big was America in 1888?

In 1888, America was growing fast. New immigrants were pouring in from Europe. Between 1850 and 1890, the population grew from 23 million to 62 million. (Today our population is 325 million.)

Back in 1888, there were only thirty-eight states, instead of the fifty we have today. Places

States and Territories of the United States of America
May 17 1884 to November 2 1889

like northern and southern Dakota, Arizona, New Mexico, and Utah were called "territories." These were areas controlled by the US government. The people there had to follow most US laws. But they didn't have the same rights as people living in states. For example, they could not cast a vote for president.

Originally known as "Dakota Territory," North and South Dakota became states in 1889. It wasn't until 1959 that America had fifty states. Alaska and Hawaii were the last to be admitted.

Today, there are still American territories, including Puerto Rico, the US Virgin Islands in the Caribbean, and the Pacific islands of Guam, the Mariana Islands, and American Samoa.

Did the grasshopper attacks really happen?

Yes! Also known as locusts, these insects terrorized people and destroyed farms throughout the late 1800s and early 1900s. They were also known

The Rocky
Mountain locust

as "grasshopper plagues." The insects came from the west, in the Rocky Mountains. They attacked farms on prairies from Dakota down to northern Texas and all the way west to California.

The gigantic swarms could be miles wide. The largest, which attacked the prairie, was 1,800 miles long and 110 miles wide. Yes, *miles*. That is larger than all the New England states put together, plus New York, Maryland, and Pennsylvania. The swarms consisted of one particular species of insect: the Rocky Mountain locust. They were brown and grew to be about an inch long. Scientists believe they were attracted by the wheat and corn the farmers were growing. They devoured everything that grew. They'd also eat saddles, wooden fences, and laundry hanging out to dry.

There was nothing that could be done to stop these attacks, which mostly happened in the summer. People tried everything. Farmers set fire to their fields. In 1877, the governor of Minnesota even ordered a statewide day of prayer to stop them. Farmers used "hopperdozers," which were giant metal devices covered with tar, oil, and molasses that they dragged through the fields to capture the grasshoppers.

Nothing worked.

Then, in the early 1900s, the grasshopper attacks suddenly stopped. The Rocky Mountain locust became extinct. There are still giant locust swarms in America and around the world. But none are as gigantic and destructive as those that attacked across the prairie in the 1800s.

If life was so hard on the prairie in the 1880s, why did so many people want to move there?

After the Civil War ended, in 1865, the US government wanted more farmers to move west. And what better way to lure people than to give away land for free?

In 1862, our government passed a new law: the Homestead Act. It said that any man or single woman over the age of twenty-one could have 160 acres of land (about one-quarter mile) for free. All a person had to do was pay ten dollars, fill out a form, and work the land for five years.

Back then, owning a farm was a dream for millions of Americans, people like John's parents. And the offer of free land out west was simply too good to pass up. Few could imagine just how hard life would be.

What happened to the Native American people who had been living on the prairie?

The story of what happened to America's native peoples is one of the most shameful in our history.

There are more than 550 different nations or tribes in America. Each has a unique culture and language.

When Christopher Columbus first arrived in America, there were millions of native people already living here (nobody knows the exact number, but some experts say there were ten million people or more). Native peoples had been living throughout America for thousands of years.

The people who were living on the prairie before the settlers arrived were members of the Sioux nation. There are seven different Sioux tribes.

The Sioux way of life at that time depended mostly on hunting buffalo (also known as *bison*). Up until the 1800s, there were millions and millions of these big, shaggy animals living on the prairie. The Sioux hunted them in the fall, and used almost every part of the animals they killed. They ate the meat, turned the fur into warm blankets and robes, the hides into shoes and tents. They carved the bones to make tools and shovels. Nothing was wasted.

When settlers started moving in and building farms, they began killing the buffalo. The big herds trampled crops and got in the way of the railroads being built. The United States Army helped kill the buffalo. By the 1880s, almost all of them were gone. This was a catastrophe for the Sioux; many people starved to death.

But the loss of the buffalo was only one of many problems for the Sioux. Many died of diseases brought by the settlers. There were terrible battles with the US Army. Sioux warriors attacked settlers, and settlers attacked the Sioux. Fear and anger spread.

By 1888, at the time of the blizzard, the American government had forced the Sioux to move to "reservations," land set aside just for them. This land was generally not good for farming or for hunting. Many more people starved.

What happened to the Sioux people happened to native peoples all over America. Their lands were taken. Their way of life was destroyed.

Today, there are roughly 5.2 million Native American people in the United States. Some live on reservations, but most live and work and go to schools in cities and towns throughout America.

FOR FURTHER READING AND LEARNING

To learn more about settlers like John and his family:

Children of the Wild West, by Russell Freedman, Clarion Books, 1983

Hattie Big Sky, by Kirby Larson, Random House, 2006

Our Only May Amelia, by Jennifer L. Holm, HarperCollins, 1999

To learn more about Sioux people:

The Christmas Coat: Memories of My Sioux

Childhood, by Virginia Driving Hawk Sneve, Holiday House, 2011

   Greet the Dawn: The Lakota Way, by S. D. Nelson, South Dakota State Historical Society, 2012

   Indian Boyhood, by Charles A. Eastman, 1902; Dover paperback, 1971

My favorite book about a blizzard is about the other blizzard of 1888, the one that hit the East Coast, including New York City:

   Blizzard! The Storm That Changed America, by Jim Murphy, Scholastic, 2000

SELECTED BIBLIOGRAPHY

Buggies, Blizzards, and Babies, by Cora Frear Hawkins, Iowa State University Press, 1st edition, 1971

The Children's Blizzard, by David Laskin, HarperCollins, 2004

A Good Year to Die: The Story of the Great Sioux War, by Charles M. Robinson III, Random House, 1995

Harvest of Grief: Grasshopper Plagues and Public Assistance in Minnesota, 1873–78, by Annette Atkins, Minnesota Historical Society Press, 1984

A History of US: Book 7: Reconstruction and Reform (1865–1896), by Joy Hakim, 2nd edition, Oxford University Press paperback, 1999

Indian Boyhood, by Charles A. Eastman, 1902; Dover paperback, 1971

Letters of a Woman Homesteader, by Elinore Pruitt Stewart, with illustrations by N. C. Wyeth, Mariner/Houghton Mifflin paperback, 1988

No Time on My Hands, by Grace Snyder, Bison Books/University of Nebraska Press, 1986

Old Rail Fence Corners: Frontier Tales Told by Minnesota Pioneers, by Daughters of the American Revolution, edited by Lucy L. W. Morris, Publications of the Minnesota Historical Society, reprint edition, 1976

Pioneer Women: Voices from the Kansas Frontier, by Joanna L. Stratton, with an introduction by Arthur M. Schlesinger Jr., Simon & Schuster, 1st Touchstone edition, 1982

Rachel Calof's Story: Jewish Homesteader on the Northern Plains, by Rachel Calof, edited by

J. Sanford Rikoon, Indiana University Press, 1995

Undaunted Courage, by Stephen E. Ambrose, Simon & Schuster, 1996

The Worst Hard Time: The Untold Story of Those Who Survived the Great American Dust Bowl, by Timothy Egan, Houghton Mifflin, 2006

ACKNOWLEDGMENTS

Special thanks to Devon Ward and Marlene Burr Ward, and to the Blue Earth County Historical Society in Mankato, Minnesota; the Center for Western Studies in Sioux Falls, South Dakota; the Minnesota History Museum in St. Paul, Minnesota; and the Jerauld County Pioneer Museum in Wessington, South Dakota, for providing me with primary source materials — articles, journals, and photographs — that helped me in my research.

I SURVIVED

When disaster strikes, heroes are made.

Read the bestselling series by Lauren Tarshis!

Join the Historians Club at **scholastic.com/isurvived**